preserves

JAMS, PICKLES, AND LIQUEURS

preserves

JAMS, PICKLES, AND LIQUEURS

LINDY WILDSMITH

PHOTOGRAPHY BY TARA FISHER

RYLAND
PETERS
& SMALL

LONDON NEW YORK

Senior Designer	Paul Tilby
Commissioning Editor	Elsa Petersen-Schepelern
Editor	Susan Stuck
Production	Patricia Harrington
Art Director	Gabriella Le Grazie
Publishing Director	Alison Starling
Food Stylist	Bridget Sargeson
Props Stylist	Chloe Brown

First published in the United States in 2004
by Ryland Peters & Small, Inc.
519 Broadway, 5th Floor
New York, NY 10012
www.rylandpeters.com

10 9 8 7 6 5 4 3 2 1

Library of Congress Cataloging-in-Publication Data

Wildsmith, Lindy.
 Preserves : jams, pickles, and liqueurs / Lindy Wildsmith ;
photography by Tara Fisher.
    p. cm.
 Includes index.
 ISBN 1-84172-715-6
 1. Canning and preserving. I. Title.
 TX601.W65 2004
 641.4--dc22
                2004000994

CONTENTS

INTRODUCTION 6

JAMS, JELLIES, AND MARMALADES 10

PRESERVED FRUITS 34

LIQUEURS 40

PICKLES AND CHUTNEYS 48

INDEX 64

introduction

For the uninitiated, preserving can be intimidating. To begin, it has its own vocabulary—pectin, setting point, boiling-water bath, Mason jars, screw bands, canners. It sounds like a trip to your great-grandmother's kitchen.

Then there's the time factor. Preserving can be an all-day affair. But not necessarily—after you get into the swing of preserving, you can put up a few or several jars of preserves in about an hour. And it can be a lot of fun.

Mastering the basic recipes is simple and the temptation to preserve every fruit and vegetable in sight can become irresistible. If you don't grow your own, homemade preserves can cost two or three times the supermarket equivalent. But the sheer pleasure of preparing and eating them makes it all worthwhile. Your work sits on the shelf seductively maturing, promising the taste and essence of summer.

Jams are made with whole fruit, marmalades with the zest of citrus fruit, and jellies with the juice of the fruit. Pickles and chutneys are made with fruit and vegetables preserved in vinegars. Fruit can also be preserved in liquor as an after-dinner treat, in vinegar to create interesting pickles, salted for use in cooking, or made into liqueurs.

If you can bear the wait, leave your jams and chutneys to mature for at least a month, while pickles are best kept three months. Liqueurs should be left for twelve months.

The English are famous the world over for fine preserves, teas, and porcelain and the history of all three is intertwined. The Museum of Worcester Porcelain has a fascinating collection of early (1760) blue-and-white, leaf-shaped, underglaze pickle dishes. This was not culinary affectation—they were made because the vinegar in pickles attacked other porcelain finishes. Pickle dishes were made in sets and sat center table to accommodate the wide range of sweet and savory pickles so popular at the time, not least of all to pep up otherwise dreary food. Each place setting had its own dish, as they do today in a Chinese restaurant.

GENERAL PRESERVING EXPLAINED

EQUIPMENT: A large, wide, heavy pan; a long wooden spoon; a ladle; Mason jars with screw bands and new lids; a stockpot or canner; and labels—these are all you need. Plus a spice bag for flavorings and a skimmer are handy too. A candy thermometer may also be useful, as would a jam funnel, but I have neither. For jellies, you need a jelly bag. You can buy stands for them, but I use an S-hook suspended from a pantry door.

FRUIT AND VEGETABLES: Choose only good quality produce in peak condition. Do not use overripe fruit. If you grow your own, use produce as it matures, not when it is past its best. Windfall hard fruits such as apples or pears can be used: wash the fruit well and cut away the bruised parts. After you have mastered the basics, you can experiment with any produce, spices, herbs, and nuts.

QUANTITIES: Before refrigeration, preserving was the only means of bringing variety to the table out of season. As recently as the 1950s and 60s, thrifty folks grew produce to make preserves to keep them going through the winter. Old recipes were for large quantities, but you can use as little as 1 pound of fruit and sugar. This will make only a jar or two, but it won't take long to prepare, cook, and set. Transfer the scrapings of the jam pan to a small dish to sample on toast for breakfast next morning (cook's perks). If it hasn't set, it is not too late to boil it up again.

JARS AND LIDS: Keep a plentiful supply of canning jars, screw bands, and new lids ready for use. Canning jars, also called Mason jars, come in ½-pint, 1-pint, 1½-pint, and 1-quart sizes. The smaller jars are good for jams, small pickles, and chutneys, and the quart jars for preserved and pickled fruits. The lid—called "dome," "self-sealing," or "snap" by the individual manufacturers—is a metal disk with a rim that sits neatly on the jar. The rim's underside has a rubbery sealing compound. The center surface is enameled. Always use new lids when preserving. Jars and screw bands can be reused.

PREPARING JARS FOR CANNING: Wash the jars (even new ones), screw bands, and lids in hot, soapy water. Rinse well with scalding water. Put the lids in a small pan, add water to cover, and bring to a simmer. Leave the lids in the pan until ready to use. Boil a kettle of water. Put the jars on a clean dishtowel in the sink or on the counter; set the jars on the towel and fill with boiling hot water. Leave filled until ready to use. This protects from dust or airborne microbes.

FINISHING TOUCHES

Collect tiny fabric remnants and funky papers to tie over the lids—6-inch squares at most—plus a pair of pinking shears to finish the edges. You can write on paper covers to eliminate labels. Lengths of string, twine, cord, ribbon, thread, wire, or wool all make good ties.

JAM, JELLY, and MARMALADE MAKING EXPLAINED

PECTIN: All fruit contains pectin in the cell walls and it is this pectin that sets preserves. Apples and lemons are pectin rich, strawberries and blackberries are pectin poor, and other fruits stand somewhere in the middle. Apple jelly sets exceptionally well, blackberry jelly does not—combine the two and you will have a really good set. For pectin to work, it needs some acid. Equally, mix strawberries and lemon juice, and your jam will set well. If in doubt about the level of pectin in your fruit, simply add the juice of half a lemon to every pound of fruit. An acid note will add a sharp tone to the sweet flavor of the jams. Commercially produced pectin can be added for a thick set; follow manufacturer's guidelines. I prefer the natural set created by pectin-rich fruit. The pectin level in fruit is at its highest when the fruit is only just ripe and still firm; pectin diminishes the riper the fruit. This is why it is essential to use fruit in peak condition, slightly underripe rather than overripe.

TESTING FOR PECTIN: You can test for pectin by mixing 1 teaspoon of the cooked fruit juice with 1 tablespoon rubbing alcohol in a small bowl. Swish the mixture around for a minute and look for a clot. If there is a large, well-formed clot, the pectin content is high. If there are scattered clots, the pectin level is medium. If there are a few dots, the pectin content is low. Do not taste this sample—it's poisonous.

PRE-COOKING THE FRUIT: Soft fruits such as raspberries, blackberries, and strawberries require little pre-cooking but fruit such as apricots, plums, figs, pears, and apples must be simmered gently in water until soft before adding the sugar. The longer you cook the fruit, the softer it becomes, and if you do not like whole fruit in your jam, simply mash the cooked fruit to reduce it to pulp. Remember, the more water added to the fruit, the longer the reduction time.

SUGAR: Should be added over very low heat, and stirred into the fruit until dissolved, otherwise it will become hard and burn.

SETTING: When the fruit is soft, the water reduced, and sugar dissolved, increase the heat and boil hard. At first the bubbles will be small, white, and frothy, but as the liquid reduces, the bubbles become larger and the fruit color starts to show through.

When the bubbles have a caramel look to them, the jelling or setting point is near.

TESTING FOR SET: Always put a saucer and 2–3 teaspoons in the refrigerator or freezer to cool before you start jam making. Boil the reduced preserve hard for 5 minutes, take the pan off the heat, and test for set. Take a teaspoon of the preserve, put it on the cold saucer in the refrigerator or freezer, and leave for 5 minutes. Push it with a finger—if it offers resistance or crinkles, it is ready. If it is still liquid, return to the heat, boil a few minutes longer, and test again. Do not leave the pan boiling while testing. Your jam will overcook, become caramelized, sticky, lose its color, or burn. Just be patient, pull the pan off the heat, and wait a few minutes. Alternatively, use a candy thermometer to gauge the setting point (220°F). (For cooks at higher altitudes, the setting point is 8°F higher than the boiling point of water at your altitude.)

SKIMMING: Scum forms on jams and jellies while boiling. Don't remove it until setting point has been reached and the heat turned off. Scum keeps forming during cooking, so do it once at the end. Use a flat, perforated skimmer.

FILLING JARS: When the preserve is cooked, dump out the water from the jars and ladle in the preserve. Fill the jars almost to the top, leaving leeway or headroom as specified by the recipe. Headroom allows for expansion or bubbling up of the preserve during processing. Wipe the rim and threads of the jar with a damp paper towel. Put the lids on the jars and twist on the screw bands firmly, but not too tightly.

PROCESSING JARS IN A BOILING-WATER BATH: For a lasting seal, preserves and pickles should be processed in a boiling-water bath. A large pot called a canner, a rack, and jar lifter are often sold as a unit for this task. You can improvise with a large stockpot, a lid, a heatproof plate, and clean dishtowels.

If you have a canner, put the rack in the base, set the jars in the rack, and add water to cover the tops of the jars by 2 inches. Cover the canner.

If using a stockpot, put a folded dishtowel in the base of the pot. Set the filled jars on top and put more folded towels around the jars to prevent them from banging while the water is boiling. Lay another towel on top and weight it down with a heatproof plate. Fill the pot with water to cover the tops of the jars by 2 inches. Cover the pot.

Bring the water in the canner or stockpot slowly to a boil. When the water reaches a boil, set a timer for the processing time recommended by the recipe. When done, carefully lift the jars from the pot and set on a dish towel. As the jars cool, you will probably hear the metal lid making a faint "plink" as the lid becomes concave, indicating that the jar is sealed.

When the jars have cooled, label with date and contents, then store in a cool, dark pantry.

YIELD: It is quite difficult to be accurate as to how much preserve you will end up with—one pound of fruit tends to yield a pint of jam, more marmalade, and less jelly. It's impossible to judge, so be flexible.

AN EXTRA NOTE FOR JELLY MAKERS

Jellies are made with the fruit juices simmered in water, then drained in a jelly bag overnight. It is tempting to stint on the water—many recipes suggest using pure fruit juice. However this can produce a disappointing yield. Scald the jelly bag with boiling water before adding the fruit. Then the fabric absorbs water, not juice. Never squeeze the bag, as this causes the jelly to cloud. Instead, leave to drip naturally overnight. When drained, simply measure the juice and add 2 cups sugar to every 2½ cups juice. Apples and crabapples yield well and make easy jellies for a first experiment.

WHAT CAN GO WRONG

The most common fault is not getting a good set. If you discover after potting that your jam has not quite set, don't worry. When you have half an hour to spare, return the jam to the pan, boil it again slowly, and then boil hard for a few minutes, and test for set. You must of course wash the jars and screw bands again and use fresh lids when re-potting. If a tiny piece of fruit catches on the base of the pan, take it out and continue. If more has caught, transfer the jam to a clean pan and continue. If your jam crystallizes, it is because you boiled the sugar before it dissolved or you used too much sugar. There is nothing to do but start again. If you over-boil jam and it becomes hard and sticky or burns—forget it.

PRESERVED FRUITS EXPLAINED

There are many ways of preserving whole fruit; here I deal only with the use of liquor, vinegars, and spices, which are all natural preservatives. There are many kinds of jars and bottles from ½ pint to 3–4 quart capacities—follow manufacturer's instructions. However, because the recipes in this section use alcohol or vinegar to preserve the fruit, jars do not need processing after filling. If stems are still attached to pears, cherries, plums, or other fruits, preserve them as well. Tuck whole spices such as star anise on the outside of the fruit where it shows through the glass—this gives preserves a professional look. Preserved fruits keep well for 6 months to a year, but once opened must be eaten immediately.

LIQUEUR MAKING EXPLAINED

There is fun and magic to liqueur making evoking both childhood games and the alchemist's art. There is little preparation, simply steeping and shaking the fruit with liquor and sugar, then waiting 12 months or longer until your brew is perfectly matured. Liqueurs were highly regarded not only as drinks, but also as medicines, and every household had its secret recipe. They are served after a meal because they aid digestion. Use any colorless liquor, such as gin, rum, or vodka—or brandy.

EQUIPMENT: You will need a ready supply of large, clean, glass jars with screwtop lids for steeping the fruit, a large plastic funnel, a pack of large-size coffee filter papers, a mortar and pestle, a jelly bag, a selection of interesting screwtop or corked bottles, adhesive labels, and, of course, an elegant decanter and glasses.

PICKLE and CHUTNEY MAKING EXPLAINED

Pickles are fruits and vegetables preserved in vinegar and spices. Chutneys are chopped, cooked slowly with vinegar and spices, and packed closely into jars. Push pickles down with the handle of a wooden spoon and then fill up with vinegar. Check jars for air bubbles before sealing—slide a clean knife blade down the side of the jar to release them. Raw pickles should be kept at least 3 months before opening. Cooked pickles and chutney may be eaten after one month. After opening, they should be used quickly.

JAMS, JELLIES, AND MARMALADES

B e sure to read Jam, Jelly, and Marmalade Making Explained (page 7) before starting a recipe.

Dried apricot conserve

Apricots make one of the most luxurious preserves of all. It can be made with dried as well as fresh apricots. Dried apricots need soaking well, then long, slow cooking to soften the skins. The apricot season is fairly short and if, like me, you love apricots and find it difficult to resist eating them, you might find this recipe using dried apricots very useful.

2½ cups dried apricots (soaked weight about 2 lb.)

freshly squeezed juice of 1 lemon

5 cups sugar

⅓ cup walnut pieces

2 tablespoons Amaretto liqueur (optional)

4 jam jars, ½ pint each, with screw bands and new lids, sterilized (page 7)

MAKES ABOUT 1 QUART

Cut the apricots in 4–8 pieces, put in a large bowl, cover with cold water, add the lemon juice, and set aside for 24 hours.

Strain off the juice into a large measuring cup and make up to 1 quart with cold water.

Put the fruit in a heavy pan, add the juice and water, and simmer over low heat for 30 minutes or until quite soft. The fruit can be mashed at this stage or left in pieces.

Add the sugar and bring slowly to simmering point. Cook gently, stirring until dissolved.

Increase the heat and boil hard for 10 minutes, add the walnut pieces, return to a fast boil, and test for set (page 8).

If the jam is not ready, put the pan back on the heat to boil for a few minutes longer and test again. Repeat this process if necessary and remember to take the jam off the heat while testing, because over-boiling will ruin it.

When setting point has been reached, add the Amaretto to the pan, return to a boil, stir, and skim if necessary. Let the jam rest for 20 minutes, then stir well, and ladle into hot jars, leaving ¼ inch headroom. Wipe the rims with a damp paper towel and cap the jars. Process for 10 minutes in a boiling-water bath (page 8). Let cool, label, and store in a cool, dark pantry until required.

VARIATION **Fresh apricot preserve**

Cut 2 lb. fresh apricots into 4–8 pieces, remove the pits, but do not discard. Put the fruit in a large pan, add ⅔ cup water and the lemon juice, and cook until quite soft. Crack 12 apricot pits and take out the kernels. Blanch the kernels in boiling water, remove the skins, and pat dry. Proceed as for the main recipe, adding the apricot kernels instead of the walnuts.

Dolly's strawberry jam

Dolly Nash was an old family friend, "a county woman" as my Mother liked to call her, even though she came from far-away Tasmania. As a child in the 1950s, I loved visiting her picturebook farmhouse—the low-ceilinged bedrooms and high beds with feather mattresses were straight out of a fairy story, as was Dolly's Strawberry Jam.

2 lb. small strawberries, picked in dry weather (8 cups)

freshly squeezed juice of 1 lemon

5 cups sugar

3-4 jam jars, ½ pint each, with screw bands and new lids, sterilized (page 7)

MAKES ABOUT 1 QUART

Wash the fruit if necessary and pat dry. Hull the strawberries and discard any that are not in perfect condition. Put in a large pan and cook gently over very low heat just for a few minutes to start the juices running. Take care not to let the fruit burn. Let stand overnight. If you like, the fruit can be mashed at this stage.

Add the lemon juice and sugar to the fruit and bring to simmering point over low heat. Stir well while the sugar is dissolving. When the sugar has dissolved, increase the heat and boil rapidly for 10 minutes (remember to stir occasionally to make sure the pan does not burn), until the juice has reduced and the jam starts to thicken.

Take the pan off the heat and test for set (page 8). If the jam is not ready, put the pan back on the heat to boil for a few minutes longer and test again. Repeat this process if necessary and remember to take the jam off the heat while testing, because over-boiling will ruin it.

When setting point has been reached, skim the jam with a perforated skimmer, stir it well, and let stand for 20 minutes for the fruit to settle. Stir and ladle into into hot jars, leaving ¼ inch headroom. Wipe the rims with a damp paper towel and cap the jars. Process for 5 minutes in a boiling-water bath (page 8). Let cool, label, and store in a cool, dark pantry until required.

VARIATION **Strawberry jam with balsamic vinegar**

If you have a taste for strawberries with balsamic vinegar, here is a foolproof, adult recipe. I love it on toast for breakfast or with biscuits and cream, but it also makes yummy little tarts topped with whipped cream, or try it melted on ice cream in tall glasses.

Follow the instructions for the main recipe, but omit the lemon juice and, rather than cooking the fruit first, put in a bowl, add the sugar and ⅔ cup balsamic vinegar, cover with a clean cloth, and let steep overnight. Stir from time to time.

Italian fig conserve

Italian jams are traditionally made with slightly less sugar than other jams; say eight parts sugar to ten parts fruit, rather than the usual equal parts. This is because peaches, apricots, figs, and other typically Mediterranean fruits are sweet compared with temperate soft fruits and plums, which are acidic and require more sugar.

Make sure you use only plump, firm fruit. You can use green figs, but they should be peeled first. It is perfect with crusty bread and butter, brioche, or toast for breakfast, but would also make excellent jam tartlets or Italian *crostata*. There is also a trend in the Veneto region of Italy to serve some of their more unusual cheeses with honey or fruit preserves.

Wipe the figs and chop into tiny pieces. Put in a pan with the lemon juice and a scant 1 cup water. Cook over low heat until soft—this make take 20–30 minutes, but if the skins are not cooked until tender at this stage, they will be tough when boiled with the sugar. Add the sugar and cook over low heat until dissolved. Stir in the vanilla, increase the heat, and boil until setting point is reached (page 8), 5–10 minutes.

If the jam is not ready, put the pan back on the heat to boil for a few minutes longer and test again. Repeat this process if necessary and remember to take the jam off the heat while testing, because over-boiling will ruin it.

When setting point has been reached, skim the jam with a perforated skimmer, stir it well, and let stand for 20 minutes for the fruit to settle. Stir and ladle into hot jars, leaving ½ inch headroom. Wipe the rims with a damp paper towel and cap the jars. Process for 5 minutes in a boiling-water bath (page 8). Let cool, label, and store in a cool, dark pantry until required.

VARIATION Try experimenting with peaches, nectarines, and kiwifruit, although it may not be necessary to cook the fruit for so long.

3 lb. fresh firm black Mission figs, about 36

freshly squeezed juice of 2 lemons

6 cups sugar

½ tablespoon pure vanilla extract (optional)

3–4 jam jars, ½ pint each, with screw bands and new lids, sterilized (page 7)

MAKES ABOUT 1 QUART

Greengage jam

I love the combination of plums and aniseed, whether for jam, chutney, bottling, stewing, pies, crumbles, or fools. Cinnamon and cloves also work well if aniseed is not a favorite of yours. Greengages make a dark golden-yellow jam; other plum varieties will make jams that vary in color from yellow to pink or purple.

3 lb. greengages or other plums (8 cups sliced)

1 large whole star anise

7½ cups sugar

2–4 jam jars, ½ pint each, with screw bands and new lids, sterilized (page 7)

MAKES 1 PINT–1 QUART

Rinse the fruit, remove the stalks, and let dry naturally in the sun. Put the fruit in a large pan with the star anise and ½ cup water and simmer gently to soften the skins, taking care not to let the fruit become mushy.

Discard the star anise. Add the sugar and continue to simmer over low heat to dissolve the sugar, stirring all the time. Bring to a boil and remove as many pits as come to the surface. Boil rapidly until setting point is reached (page 8), 5–10 minutes.

If the jam is not ready, put the pan back on the heat to boil for a few minutes longer and test again. Repeat this process if necessary and remember to take the jam off the heat while testing, because over-boiling will ruin it.

When setting point has been reached, skim the jam with a perforated skimmer, stir it well, and let stand for 20 minutes for the fruit to settle. Stir and ladle into hot jars, leaving ½ inch headroom. Wipe the rims with a damp paper towel and cap the jars. Process for 5 minutes in a boiling-water bath (page 8).

Let cool, label, and store in a cool, dark pantry until required.

VARIATION **Victoria plum jam**

If using large plum varieties such as Victoria, it may be a good idea to cut the plums in half and remove the pits before cooking.

Pineapple and apple jam

This jam is very refreshing and the prettiest shade of lemon yellow. If you are crazy about pineapple, it could be good eaten straight off the spoon, Mediterranean style. Who needs bread? Try perking up some vanilla ice cream with a few spoons of jam and a splash of rum. You could even paint a little rum on the inside of the lid before sealing the jars, just to give the jam a deliciously tropical taste.

4 cups pineapple flesh (2 fresh pineapples)

2 large tart apples, such as Granny Smith

freshly squeezed juice of 1½ lemons

8 green cardamom pods (optional)

5 cups sugar

3-4 jam jars, ½ pint each, with screw bands and new lids, sterilized (page 7)

MAKES ABOUT 1 QUART

If using whole pineapples, peel and core first. Cut out the "eyes" with the end of a sharp knife or vegetable peeler. Peel and core the apples. Cut the pineapple and apples into tiny chunks. Put the fruit in a large pan, sprinkle with lemon juice, and set aside. Add ⅔ cup water to the fruit and simmer over low heat until the apple softens, 20–30 minutes. Meanwhile, split open the cardamom pods, take out the seeds, and crush them with a mortar and pestle. Add to the fruit as it cooks.

Add the sugar to the pan and continue to cook over low heat until the sugar has dissolved, stirring all the while. Increase the heat and boil rapidly until setting point is reached (page 8). This will take 5–10 minutes.

If the jam is not ready, put the pan back on the heat to boil for a few minutes longer and test again. Repeat this process if necessary and remember to take the jam off the heat while testing, because over-boiling will ruin it.

When setting point has been reached, skim the jam with a perforated skimmer, stir it well, and let stand for 20 minutes for the fruit to settle. Stir and ladle into hot jars, leaving ½ inch headroom. Wipe the rims with a damp paper towel and cap the jars. Process for 5 minutes in a boiling-water bath (page 8).

Let cool, label, and store in a cool, dark pantry until required.

VARIATION Try experimenting with mangoes and other tropical fruit. Don't forget to add the apples, because they will help the jam set.

Rhubarb and ginger jam

This is a robust jam that deserves a place alongside the zingiest of marmalades. Choose young pink rhubarb if possible, because it will give lovely pink color to the jam—green rhubarb tends to turn brown when cooked. However, the flavor is just as good whatever the color. This would also make a delicious old-fashioned dessert such as jam tart or steamed jam pudding.

3 lb. young pink rhubarb, about 12 cups chopped

7½ cups sugar

grated zest and freshly squeezed juice of 1½ unwaxed lemons

1–1½ oz. fresh ginger, peeled, to taste

3–4 jam jars, ½ pint each, with screw bands and new lids, sterilized (page 7)

MAKES ABOUT 1 QUART

Wipe the rhubarb, trim it, cut into chunks, and put in a bowl with the sugar, lemon zest, and juice. Cover and let stand overnight.

Crush the ginger with a mortar and pestle or blender and add to the fruit and sugar. Transfer to a large pan and bring slowly to simmering point, stirring all the time to dissolve the sugar. Simmer gently until the fruit has softened, then increase the heat and boil rapidly for 5–10 minutes until setting point is reached (page 8).

If the jam is not ready, put the pan back on the heat to boil for a few minutes longer and test again. Repeat this process if necessary and remember to take the jam off the heat while testing, because over-boiling will ruin it.

When setting point has been reached, skim the jam with a perforated skimmer, stir it well, and let stand for 20 minutes for the fruit to settle. Stir and ladle into hot jars, leaving ½ inch headroom. Wipe the rims with a damp paper towel and cap the jars. Process for 5 minutes in a boiling-water bath (page 8).

Let cool, label, and store in a cool, dark pantry until required.

VARIATION **Raspberry and rhubarb jam**

Rhubarb combines well with soft fruit such as raspberries and strawberries, giving them more body and reducing the seediness of the fruit. Use half soft fruit and half rhubarb, and omit the ginger.

Apple jelly with lemon and sage

My Brazilian friend Melodie is famous for her apple jelly, which she makes from windfall apples. She took me through the method from orchard to table in an animated monologue totally devoid of weights and measures or times.

3 lb. apples, any variety (cleaned weight)

water (see method)

sugar (see method)

freshly squeezed juice of 1½ lemons

a large bunch of sage or mint tied up tightly leaving a long piece of twine free

a few extra sage leaves for decoration

a jelly bag or cheesecloth

2-3 jam jars, ½ pint each, with screw bands and new lids, sterilized (page 7)

MAKES 1-1½ PINTS

Peel, core, and chop the apples. Put them in a large pan and add enough water so that if you peer in, you can just see the water level appearing under the fruit. Partially cover with a lid and boil slowly until the fruit forms a pulp, 1–1½ hours.

Transfer the fruit pulp to a jelly bag suspended over a large bowl. (Melodie uses the legs of an upturned kitchen chair. I use an S-hook hung from a pantry door.) Leave to drip all night. Do not be tempted to squeeze the bag, because this will make the jelly cloudy.

Measure the quantity of juice obtained. Pour it into a large pan. Add 1 scant cup sugar for every 1 cup juice. Add the lemon juice. Set the pan over low heat and slowly dissolve the sugar, stirring all the while. When the sugar has dissolved, tie the bunch of sage to the handle of the pan and suspend in the jelly. Boil rapidly for 5–10 minutes until setting point is reached (page 8). Stir from time to time to make sure the pan does not burn.

If the jam is not ready, put the pan back on the heat to boil for a few minutes longer and test again. Repeat this process if necessary and remember to take the jam off the heat while testing, because over-boiling will ruin it.

When setting point has been reached, discard the bunch of sage and skim the jelly with a perforated skimmer. Stir and ladle into hot jars, leaving ½ inch headroom. Plunge a few fresh sage leaves into boiling water, pat dry, and push one leaf into each jar. Wipe the rims with a damp paper towel and cap the jars. Process for 5 minutes in a boiling-water bath (page 8).

VARIATION Other herbs such as rosemary or thyme and spices such as ginger, chile, cinnamon, or star anise can be used instead of the sage. If making chile jelly, stir in 1–2 finely chopped, seeded chiles instead of the bunch of sage.

Crabapple jelly

If you have space for a small tree in your garden, it's worth planting a crabapple. You will have pretty blossom in spring and jewel-like miniature apples in the late summer and early fall. Use them to make this stunning pink jelly to serve with roast pork, poultry, and game. Sadly, we don't have a crabapple tree, but our friend Paul has two. One produces tiny scarlet and cream, plum-shaped fruit and the other a crimson, cherry-size apple. This is his recipe.

3 lb. crabapples

1 unwaxed lemon

sugar

a jelly bag or cheesecloth

2-3 jam jars, ½ pint each, with screw bands and new lids, sterilized (page 7)

MAKES 1–1½ PINTS

Sort the crabapples, discarding any that are badly bruised or marked and any leaves that are still attached. Wash the fruit, cut them in half, and put in a large pan. Fill the pan with water to just under the level of the fruit. Peel the zest thinly from the lemon and add this and the peeled lemon to the pan. Partially cover with a lid, bring slowly to a boil, and simmer for 1 hour. Transfer to a jelly bag or cheesecloth suspended over a large bowl and leave to drip all night.

Measure the juice into a clean preserving pan and, for every 2½ cups of juice, add 2¼ cups sugar. Set over low heat and bring to simmering point, dissolving the sugar, stirring all the while. When it has dissolved, increase the heat and boil hard for 5–10 minutes until setting point is reached.

Take the pan off the heat and test for set (page 8). If the jelly is not ready, put the pan back on the heat to boil for a few minutes longer and test again. Repeat this process if necessary and remember to take it off the heat while testing, because over-boiling will ruin it.

When setting point has been reached, skim the jelly with a perforated skimmer. Stir and ladle into hot jars, leaving ¼ inch headroom. Wipe the rims with a damp paper towel and cap the jars. Process for 5 minutes in a boiling-water bath (page 8). Let cool, label, and store in a cool, dark pantry until required.

Red berry jelly

1 lb. strawberries
(4 cups)

1 lb. raspberries
(3 cups)

1 lb. loganberries or
tayberries (3½ cups)

1 lb. gooseberries
(3 cups)

freshly squeezed juice
of 1 lemon

sugar (see method)

*a jelly bag or
cheesecloth*

*2–3 jam jars, ½ pint
each, with screw bands
and new lids, sterilized
(page 7)*

MAKES 1–1½ PINTS

Berries make a marvelous seedless jam—use sweet ones like strawberries and raspberries, blackberry-raspberry crosses like tayberries or loganberries, then something sharp such as huckleberries, gooseberries, or sour cherries. In season, every other farm gateway sets out "pick-your-own" signs. Early summer is the time to enjoy these soft fruits fresh—and to make this jelly, which is delicious spread in the middle of a plain cake or dissolved in boiling water for a warming winter drink.

Put all the fruit in a large preserving pan with the lemon juice and 2 cups water and bring slowly to a boil. Partially cover with a lid and simmer until the fruit has softened, 10–15 minutes. Transfer to a jelly bag or cheesecloth suspended over a large bowl and leave to drip all night.

Measure the juice into a clean preserving pan and, for every 1 cup of juice, add 1 scant cup of sugar. Set over low heat and bring to simmering point, dissolving the sugar, stirring all the while. When it has dissolved, increase the heat and boil hard for 5–10 minutes until setting point is reached.

Take the pan off the heat and test for set (page 8). When setting point has been reached, skim the jelly with a perforated skimmer. Stir and ladle into hot jars, leaving ½ inch headroom. Wipe the rims with a damp paper towel and cap the jars. Process for 5 minutes in a boiling-water bath (page 8). Let cool, label, and store in a cool, dark pantry until required.

VARIATION **Jelly made with any single soft fruit**

Orange and kumquat marmalade

3 unwaxed navel oranges, well scrubbed

4 oz. kumquats, about ½ cup, well scrubbed

3 cups sugar

freshly squeezed juice of ½ lemon

1 tablespoon honey

a jelly bag or cheesecloth

2–3 jam jars, ½ pint each, with screw bands and new lids, sterilized (page 7)

MAKES ABOUT 1½ PINTS

Cut the orange zest into very thin strips with a sharp citrus zester. Put the zest in a large bowl and reserve. Cut away all the pith and put in a second large bowl.

Cut the orange into segments and reserve the segment skin, seeds, and central core of the orange, saving any juice. Add the orange segments and orange and lemon juices to the bowl of zest. Add the reserved skin, seeds, and core to the bowl of pith.

Cut the kumquats in half lengthwise, scrape out all the flesh, pith, and seeds with a teaspoon. Add this to the orange pith. Cut the kumquat "shells" into thin strips and add to the orange zest and segments.

Add 2 cups water to the bowl of fruit and add another 2 cups water to the pith and seeds. Cover both bowls with a clean cloth and let steep overnight or for 24 hours.

Put the pith and seeds in a medium pan and simmer, covered, over low heat for 30 minutes. Transfer to a jelly bag set over a bowl and let drain for 30 minutes. Squeeze the bag to extract the remaining liquid. You will notice that the juice on your hands is very sticky—this is the pectin extracted from the pith.

Pour the fruit, zest, and water into a large pan, then add the extracted liquid from the pith. Set over low heat, bring slowly to simmering point, and cook until the zest softens and the liquid has reduced by half.

Add the sugar to the pan and bring slowly to simmering point, cooking and stirring until the sugar has dissolved. Because the sugar content is high, this will take quite a long time. When the marmalade has become translucent, you will know the sugar has dissolved and you can increase the heat. Bring to a boil and boil rapidly until setting point is reached, 5–10 minutes.

Take the pan off the heat and test for set (page 8). If the marmalade is not ready, put the pan back on the heat to boil for a few minutes longer and test again. Repeat this process if necessary and remember to take the pan off the heat during testing because over-boiling will ruin it.

When setting point has been reached, add the honey, return to simmering point, then turn off the heat. Skim with a perforated skimmer, stir well, and let stand for 30 minutes for the fruit to settle. Stir and ladle into hot jars, leaving ½ inch headroom. Wipe the rims with a damp paper towel and cap the jars. Process for 10 minutes in a boiling-water bath (page 8).

Let cool, label, and store in a cool, dark pantry until required.

VARIATION **Mandarin and lemon marmalade**

Use 6–8 mandarins and 1 extra lemon in place of the oranges and kumquats.

Chunky lemon, lime, and grapefruit marmalade

The beauty of this marmalade is that it can be made in small quantities at any time of the year, not just when Seville oranges are in season. I have given quantities to yield two or three jars, but if you want to make it in bulk, then simply double or triple the ingredients. Cut the peel to suit your taste—thick or thin by hand, chunky or fine using a blender.

1 unwaxed lemon

1 small unwaxed pink grapefruit

1 unwaxed lime

5 cups sugar

freshly squeezed juice of ½ lemon

3 jam jars, ½ pint each, with screw bands and new lids, sterilized (page 7)

MAKES ABOUT 1½ PINTS

Scrub the fruit and pry out any stalk ends still attached. Put in a pan and cover with 2 cups cold water. Set over low heat and cook until tender—this will take 1½–2 hours. The fruit is ready when it "collapses." Lime zest is much tougher than other citrus peel, so you must make sure it is tender at this stage.

Transfer the fruit to a cutting board and leave until cool enough to handle. Cut in half, scrape out all the flesh and seeds, and add to the pan of water. Bring to a boil and simmer for 5 minutes. Cut the zest into strips as thin as possible, or put it in a blender and blend until chunky. Strain the water from the seeds and flesh and return it to the pan, adding the chopped zest and the lemon juice. Discard the seeds and debris.

Add the sugar to the pan and bring slowly to simmering point, stirring until the sugar has dissolved. Because the sugar content is high, this will take quite a long time. When the marmalade has become translucent, you will know the sugar has dissolved and you can increase the heat. Bring to a boil and boil rapidly until setting point is reached, 5–10 minutes.

Take the pan off the heat and test for set (page 8). If the marmalade is not ready, put the pan back on the heat to boil for a few minutes longer and test again. Repeat this process if necessary and remember to take the pan off the heat during testing because over-boiling will ruin it.

When setting point has been reached, return to a simmer, then turn off the heat. Skim with a perforated skimmer, stir well, and let stand for 30 minutes for the fruit to settle. Stir and ladle into hot jars, leaving ½ inch headroom. Wipe the rims with a damp paper towel and cap the jars. Process for 10 minutes in a boiling-water bath (page 8).

Let cool, label, and store in a cool, dark pantry until required.

VARIATION **Seville orange marmalade**

Use 3 lb. Seville oranges and multiply other ingredients by 3. This will yield about 8 jars.

A relish is a preserve for serving with meat or cheese. It is simple to make, delicious, and puts the storebought kind in the shade. This combination of fruit, spice, and port is truly festive and adds color and sparkle to roasts such as turkey and lamb, game dishes, baked, cured ham, and savory pies. This quantity will make enough to see you through the festive season, but should you relish the idea of year-round culinary cheer, make it in bulk.

Cranberry relish with orange zest, cinnamon, and port

1 inch cinnamon stick

6 whole cloves

3 cups fresh cranberries

peeled zest and freshly squeezed juice of 1 unwaxed orange

1¾ cups sugar

1–2 tablespoons port

a small cheesecloth bag with kitchen twine

1 jam jar, 1-pint, with screw band and new lid, sterilized (page 7)

MAKES 1 PINT

Put the cinnamon and cloves in a small cheesecloth bag and tie up with kitchen twine. Alternatively, use ¼ teaspoon ground cinnamon and a pinch of ground cloves.

Put the cranberries in a preserving pan with the zest and juice of the orange, the bag of spices, and the sugar. Simmer over low heat until the sugar dissolves and the fruit starts to pop, then boil for 5 minutes, until setting point is reached.

Take the pan off the heat and test for set (page 8). If the relish is not ready, put the pan back on the heat to boil for a few minutes longer and test again. Repeat this process if necessary and remember to take it off the heat while testing, because over-boiling will ruin it.

When setting point has been reached, discard the spice bag, stir in the port, skim the relish with a perforated skimmer, stir it well, and set aside for 20 minutes for the fruit to settle. Stir and ladle into the hot jar, leaving ½ inch headroom. Wipe the rim with a damp paper towel and cap the jar. Process for 5 minutes in a boiling-water bath (page 8). Let cool, label, and store in a cool, dark pantry until required.

PRESERVED FRUITS

Be sure to read Preserved Fruits explained (page 9) before starting a recipe.

Layered summer fruits in grappa

½ cup strawberries

½ cup raspberries

½ cup sweet cherries

1 cup sugar

clear liquor such as grappa or white rum, or brandy (see method)

1-pint preserving jar with screw band and new lid, sterilized (page 7)

MAKES 1 PINT

Where I live, we are surrounded by wonderful strawberry fields and commercial orchards set in an undulating misty landscape. Picking your own fruit is not much cheaper than buying it ready-picked direct from a grower, but as my daughter says, "Think of all the fruit you eat while you are picking!" (She should know—when they were small, I had to offer to weigh her and her brother, as well as our baskets, before we started picking our own.)

Put a layer of strawberries in the jar and sprinkle with 5 tablespoons sugar. Add a layer of raspberries and another 5 tablespoons sugar. Add the cherries and the remaining sugar, then top up the jar with enough grappa or other liquor to cover. Seal with a lid. Extra fruit can be added to the jar when the level falls.

The jar need not be filled immediately, but reopened and added to as each new fruit comes into season. Top up each layer of fruit with half its weight in sugar and enough liquor to cover the fruit each time the jar is opened. Serve with ice cream or alone, as a special dessert.

Note Blackberries and plums may also be added.

VARIATION **Layered "white" fruits with brandy**

Instead of red berries and cherries, use gooseberries, white cherries, grapes, apricots, greengages, and peaches. Greengages and apricots may be cut in half first, and peaches sliced.

Peach halves in brandy with star anise

Peach halves in brandy are a classic, but all kinds of fruits can be preserved in this way. Whole peaches can also be bottled— leave the skin on and pierce the fruit to the pit with a toothpick before poaching. They look magnificent, but take up a lot of room in the jar and consequently are best packed in 1–2 quart jars. As with all pickles and preserved fruits, after the jar has been opened, they should be used immediately, so keep this in mind. This recipe makes a lovely gift and the peaches are delicious served with ice cream or on their own as an after-dinner treat.

Put the peaches in a large bowl and cover with boiling water. Leave for 2 minutes for the skins to lift, drain off the water, and pull off the skins. Discard the water. Cut the peaches in half and poach in plenty of simmering water for 1–2 minutes until just tender. Lift out the peach halves with a perforated skimmer and drain on paper towels.

Measure 2 cups of the poaching water into a pan. Add 1½ cups sugar, dissolve over low heat, then bring to a boil, and boil for 7 minutes. Don't forget to keep an eye on it.

When the peach halves have cooled, arrange them in a heatproof dish in a single layer, cover with the boiling syrup, and leave for 24 hours.

After this time pour the syrup off the peach halves into a pan and add the remaining ½ cup sugar. Bring slowly to simmering point to dissolve the sugar, then boil for 2 minutes. Pour this back over the peaches, cool, cover with a cloth or lid, and leave for 2 more days.

After 2 days transfer the peach halves to a clean jar.

Put 1 cup of the syrup in a measuring cup and add to it an equal quantity of brandy. Pour the mixture over the peaches until covered, add the star anise on the outside of the fruit but on the inside of the glass, and keep for at least 1 month before using. Label at once.

4 firm just-ripe peaches

2 cups sugar

1 cup brandy

1 whole star anise

1-pint jar, with screw band and new lid, sterilized (page 7)

MAKES 1 PINT

VARIATION Nectarine halves, plums, cherries, and apricots can be prepared the same way but there is no need to peel them. For flavoring, use a cinnamon stick or vanilla instead of the star anise.

Pickled pears with tamarind and ginger

Pickled fruits such as these can be made with all kinds of vinegars; red and white wine, cider, perry, or rice. I have used malt vinegar because, however careful you are, some varieties of pear turn brown when preserved. The flavor is not impaired, nor the texture of fruit, but the color is a little off-putting. If you use some kind of dark vinegar, the change in color goes unnoticed. When pickling peaches, figs, quinces, and other more delicate fruits, I would suggest using white wine or other subtle vinegars. The combination of spices used in this recipe comes originally from the Middle East, but try others such as chile, dill, allspice, or coriander seed. If you are not able to find tamarind paste, simply omit it.

2 cups malt or cider vinegar (see above)

2 tablespoons finely grated fresh ginger

3 garlic cloves, crushed

3 heaping teaspoons tamarind paste (available in Asian stores and some supermarkets)

1½ teaspoons cumin seeds

a pinch of salt

1 cup soft brown sugar

2 lb. firm pears, peaches, figs, or quinces (see note)

3 jars, 1 pint each, with screw bands and new lids, sterilized (page 7)

MAKES 3 PINTS

Put the vinegar, ginger, garlic, tamarind paste, cumin seeds, salt, and sugar in a pan and bring slowly to simmering point. Cook over low heat until the sugar has dissolved, then boil for 5 minutes.

Meanwhile, peel the pears, cut in half, and pack into the hot jars. Fill with the reduced vinegar, leaving ½ inch headroom. Should the vinegar prove insufficient to cover the fruit, simply boil up extra vinegar, adding 3 tablespoons sugar to every ½ cup vinegar. Wipe the rims with a damp paper towel and cap the jars. Process in a boiling-water bath for 15 minutes. Label when cold.

Keep at least 3 months before opening. Serve with cheese at the end of a meal, or as part of a cured meat appetizer, with cold cooked meats, ham, game, or pies.

Note Peaches and figs do not need peeling—pears and quinces do.

LIQUEURS

B e sure to read Liqueur Making Explained (page 9) before starting a recipe.

Limoncello *"San Vigilio"*

I was a guest at Villa San Vigilio on Lake Garda, which boasts a famous formal Italian garden (most received an "English" makeover at the time of the Grand Tour). In this garden is a truly magnificent ancient lemon tree, so tall and so laden with huge fruit that the temptation to climb into it was overwhelming. Inspired by the sight of the wonderful tree, I was sure the family would have a recipe for Limoncello. Not so—and why should they? Garda is in the north of Italy and this is a drink from Campania. However, one of my hosts was from Naples and he promised to provide a recipe via his good friend, "a fantastic Neapolitan cook, Fabrizia Gerli," and this is it.

4-5 unwaxed lemons, 1 of which should be greenish

2 cups clear liquor, such as gin, grappa, vodka, or white rum

¾ cup sugar

1 screwtop jar, about 1 quart, with wide neck

1 funnel

1 clean, dry bottle, 750 ml

1 coffee filter paper

1 cork

MAKES 3 CUPS

Remove all the lemon zest with a small, sharp knife, making sure there is no white pith whatsoever. Put the zest in a large, clean, screwtop jar, then add the liquor of your choice. Cover with plastic wrap and seal with a screwtop lid. Put in a dark place for 7–10 days, shaking the jar from time to time.

To make a syrup, put the sugar and 1 cup water in a pan and boil it for 6–7 minutes. Let cool. Pour the liquor off the zest and mix with the cooled syrup. (Discard the zest or cut it into fine strips, freeze, and serve on sherbets and water ices, or in gin and tonic.) Put a funnel in the neck of the bottle and a coffee filter paper in the funnel. Carefully strain the liquor into the bottle, seal with a cork, and put it back in the dark. It will be ready to drink after 1 week.

When the limoncello is ready to drink, it can be stored in the freezer—the alcohol content will stop it from freezing. Serve from the freezer.

Orange shrub

Of all the recipes in this section of the book, shrub is the simplest to make. Traditionally, it can be made with any kind of citrus fruit, so try experimenting with grapefruit, lime, and lemon for a change. It is advisable to use unwaxed fruit, but not essential. Some shrub recipes contain wine, but the essential ingredient seems to be citrus fruit. Because there is always a ready supply of citrus, this is one drink that can be made whenever the spirit moves you, if you will forgive the pun.

Put the rum, orange zest and juice, and sugar in the jar, cover with plastic wrap, then seal with a screwtop lid. Set aside for 30 days, label with the date as a reminder, and shake 2–3 times daily.

After 30 days, strain into the bottle through a coffee filter paper set in a funnel. Cork the bottle. Although it should be kept for about 3 months in a cool, dark pantry, it is delicious served immediately. Keep in the refrigerator and serve chilled.

3 cups white rum or brandy

finely grated zest of 2 unwaxed oranges and ½ cup juice

1 cup sugar

1 screwtop jar, about 1 quart, with wide neck

1 clean dry bottle, 1-quart

1 coffee filter paper

1 funnel

1 cork

MAKES 1 QUART

Kumquat and saffron rosolio

The combination of citrus and saffron creates a splendid golden hue that glows in the sunshine while the elixir is steeping. The color alone is reason enough to make it—and if you can acquire some unusual bottles to put it in, rosolio makes an exciting gift. If you are not keen on grappa, use gin or some other colorless liquor. Do not use brandy or dark rum, because this will spoil the color. Oranges or mandarins can be used instead of kumquats.

3-5 kumquats

1 cup grappa

a good pinch of saffron threads

1¾ cups sugar

2 large screwtop jars, 1 pint each

1 clean dry bottle, 1-quart

1 coffee filter paper

1 funnel

1 cork

MAKES 1 QUART

Cut the kumquats in half lengthwise, scoop out the flesh and seeds with a spoon, then scrape out all the pith. Discard everything except the kumquat "shells." Put these in a large, clean jar. Add the grappa and saffron, then seal with a round of wax paper tied down with a rubber band.

Set the jar on a sunny windowsill for 8 days. Label with the date. Shake the jar once a day. Put the sugar and 1½ cups water in another jar, cover with plastic wrap and a screwtop lid, and leave at room temperature for 8 days, shaking it from time to time to dissolve the sugar. On the eighth day, mix the two liquids and let stand for 24 hours at room temperature.

Strain the liquid into a bottle through a coffee filter paper set in a funnel. Seal the bottle with a cork, then label and store.

Store in a dark, dry pantry at an even temperature and forget about it for at least 12 months. When you are ready to try it, pour into your best decanter and serve over ice in beautiful glasses (or straight from the freezer).

Ginger and juniper liqueur

This comes originally from the Veneto region of Italy and can be made and flavored with all kinds of seeds and spices. If you have problems finding juniper berries, try a natural food store. If using a brandy base, use a warm spice such as cinnamon or vanilla instead of juniper. This is a deliciously warming pick-me-up drink on a cold winter's day.

Peel the fresh ginger, chop it coarsely, and put in a bowl. Add the juniper berries and crush with the end of a rolling pin until both are mixed and crushed to a coarse paste. Alternatively, use a mortar and pestle.

Transfer the paste to a large, wide-necked jar, add the grappa or brandy, cover with plastic wrap, and seal with a screwtop lid. Let steep for 20 days at room temperature. Shake the jar from time to time. It's a good idea to label the bottle with the date as a reminder.

After 20 days, put the sugar and ¾ cup water in a pan and boil for 5–6 minutes until thick and syrupy. Let cool. Mix the syrup and liquor. Pour into the bottle through a coffee filter paper set in a funnel. Cork well or seal, label, and store away from direct light in a cool (frost-free) pantry for 12 months.

1 oz. fresh ginger

3 tablespoons juniper berries

2 cups grappa or brandy

1 cup sugar

1 screwtop jar, about 1 quart, with wide neck

1 clean, dry bottle, 750 ml

1 coffee filter paper

1 funnel

1 cork or seal

MAKES 3 CUPS

Country bounce

I was attracted to this recipe in an old Virginian cookbook by the following instruction, "Cheap rum at 75 or 50 cents a gallon serves equally as well as the best spirit for Bounce." What better reason for making it.

Use cherries, damsons, plums, blackberries, or elderberries and make sure your fruit is just-ripe—not under- or overripe—and never damaged.

Put the plums (including the pits) in a large bowl and pound with the end of a rolling pin. Alternatively, use a mortar and pestle.

Add the rum, cover, and let stand for 1 week at room temperature. Transfer the fruit pulp to a jelly bag set over a bowl and leave overnight to drain. Measure the quantity of juice and add 1¾ cups sugar for every 2 cups of juice. Mix well and transfer to bottles. Cork or seal.

Label and store in a cool, dark pantry for about 12 months. Filter and serve in your best decanter.

4 lb. plums,
large black cherries,
such as Bing,
or similar fruit

1 quart rum

soft brown sugar
(see method)

a jelly bag

*2 clean, dry bottles,
750 ml each*

2 corks or seals

MAKES 1½ QUARTS

Hedgerow gin

This is a classic country liqueur that can be made with almost any berry or stone fruit. The beauty is that it can be made with the rich summer and fall pickings of a country walk. Wild damsons are particularly popular, but it can be made with beach plums, elderberries, rosehips, blackberries, or blueberries—in fact all the edible fruits you find in the hedgerows.

Pack the fruit, gin, and sugar into the jar. Cover with plastic wrap and seal with a screwtop lid. Label the jar, put in a dark, dry pantry at an even temperature, and forget about it for at least 1 year.

When you are ready to try it, pour the liquor off the fruit into your best decanter, discarding (or eating) the fruit.

Don't forget, the longer you keep the liqueur the better it tastes.

1 lb. fruit

2 cups gin

2½ cups sugar

1 clean, dry, screwtop jar, about 1 quart, with wide neck

MAKES 3 CUPS

PICKLES AND CHUTNEYS

Be sure to read Pickle and Chutney Making Explained (page 9) before starting a recipe.

Layered pickled vegetables

This colorful pickle is easy to prepare and makes a delicious gift. It is tempting to keep it on show, but like most preserves it is best kept in the dark. Vary the choice of vegetables according to season and layer them according to color. Try broccoli, cauliflower, green beans, eggplant, fennel, small onions, and cucumber. If you prefer, cut the vegetables into small squares and florets and mix them up, rather than layering them. Serve as part of a mixed hors d'oeuvres with olives, cheese, and cold cuts, or add to stir-fries and casseroles.

Wash or wipe the vegetables thoroughly. Cut the bell peppers into rings, first discarding the seeds. Cut the carrots, zucchini, and celery into strips, about 2 x ½ inch.

Layer the vegetables in a colander set over a bowl, sprinkling salt on each layer. Put a weighted plate on top and let stand overnight covered with a cloth.

To make the brine, put 1¼ cups water in a pan, add the salt, vinegar, garlic, and sugar. Bring gently to a boil, then remove from the heat, cover, and let cool.

The following morning, put the vegetables in a strainer and pour boiling water over them. Drain and dry thoroughly with a clean cloth. Pack them into the jars in layers, starting with half the red bell pepper rings, half the celery

pieces, followed by half the orange bell pepper, half the zucchini, half the yellow bell pepper rings, and finishing with the remaining celery and half the carrot. Fill up each layer of vegetables with brine as you go. When the jar is full, insert the garlic, chile, and dill.

Fill the jars with brine, leaving ½ inch headroom. Check the jars for air bubbles—tap the sides to bring them to the surface or slide a thin knife blade down the inside of the jar to release them. Wipe the rims with a damp paper towel and cap the jars. Process for 15 minutes in a boiling-water bath (page 8). Leave for at least 1 week before using. Keeps for 6–12 months. After opening, the flavor of the pickles starts to deteriorate, so finish them immediately.

VARIATION **Mediterranean vegetables in oil**

Instead of brine, fill each layer with extra virgin olive oil and 1 teaspoon wine vinegar. Add blanched garlic, chile, and oregano and store in the refrigerator.

---

1 large yellow bell pepper

1 large red bell pepper

1 large orange bell pepper

2 young carrots

4 small zucchini

1 celery heart

1 garlic clove

1 fresh chile

a sprig of dill or oregano

salt

brine mix

1 tablespoon salt

⅓ cup white wine vinegar

2 teaspoons sugar

2 pickle jars, 1 pint each, with screw bands and new lids, sterilized (page 7). Choose jars that are tall and thin rather than short and wide.

MAKES 1 QUART

Moroccan preserved lemons and limes in salt

2 unwaxed lemons and 2 unwaxed limes

4 tablespoons coarse sea salt

freshly squeezed juice of 1 lemon

a clean pint jar

MAKES 1 PINT

Lemons are preserved in salt in many Eastern cultures. In Morocco, they are preserved whole, slit in quarters almost to the base. As in all preserving, whole fruits require large quantities and large jars. As smaller pieces are easier to handle, I have adapted the recipe, cutting the fruit right through into quarters, but using the traditional Moroccan method, which is very simple and requires no cooking. Salted lemons and limes can be served with roasts and fish dishes, or put a piece of lemon inside roasting poultry and baste with the salty lemon juice. Chop them up small in rice or salads, or try experimenting with tequila cocktails.

Scrub the fruit well and remove the stalk base pieces with the point of a sharp knife. Cut the lemons and limes into quarters lengthwise (taking care not to waste the juice) and put in a shallow bowl, cut sides up. Sprinkle half the salt onto the lemon flesh and let stand for 30 minutes.

Rub the salt into the fruit and pack into the jar, cut side down, pushing each wedge down well, alternating lime and lemon pieces. Fill up each layer with the remaining salt. Don't worry if the jar is over-full, because the fruit will sink as the skin softens. Leave unsealed for 3–4 days, push the fruit down, fill up with lemon juice, and seal. Keep 1 month before use.

Winter's farm pickled onions

To my horror, I have recently discovered that we have no written record of our family recipe for pickled onions, made every fall. I asked around—surely someone would have a tried-and-tested family recipe and, sure enough, I was told that "Mary makes the world's best pickled onions." However, like me, she had not made them recently and could not put her hand on the recipe. So this is a "new" recipe based on the memory of two old ones.

3 tablespoons salt

1 lb. shallots or pickling onions, such as pearl onions

spiced vinegar

8 mixed peppercorns

4 whole cloves

½ inch cinnamon stick

½ inch cube of fresh ginger

1¾ cups cup malt vinegar

1 pickle jar, 1 pint, with screw band and new lid, sterilized (page 7)

MAKES 1 PINT

To make a brine, put the salt in a pan with 2¾ cups water. Bring to a boil, remove from the heat, and let cool.

To peel the shallots, put them in a large bowl and pour boiling water over them for a few minutes. Drain, then peel.

Put the shallots in a bowl, add the cooled brine, and leave for 24 hours. After this time, drain, rinse in cold water, and dry carefully.*

To make the spiced vinegar, put the peppercorns, cloves, cinnamon, and ginger in a small pan, add the vinegar, cover, and bring to a boil over low heat. Turn off the heat, let cool, then strain.

Pack the onions into the jar, pushing them down with the handle of a wooden spoon. Fill up with the cooled spiced vinegar, leaving ½ inch headroom.

Tap the sides to remove any air bubbles or slide a thin knife blade down the inside of the jar to release them. Wipe the rim with a damp paper towel and cap the jar. Process for 15 minutes in a boiling-water bath (page 8). Store in a cool, dark pantry until required. Wait at least 3 months before tasting.

* If you would like sweet pickled onions, at this point put the onions in a bowl, sprinkle with 2 tablespoons soft brown sugar, and let stand for 24 hours, stirring from time to time to dissolve the sugar. Ladle some of the dissolved sugar into the jar with the onions before filling up with the vinegar.

Japanese pickled ginger

This is a very simple recipe for preserving fresh ginger. Traditionally, it is salted and cut into paper-thin rounds, preserved in rice vinegar, and served with sushi and other Japanese dishes. I like to cut some of the ginger into rounds and some in julienne and layer it in small jars. The ginger julienne can be served mixed with a julienne of vegetables and citrus zests to serve with roasts, marinated fish dishes, and all kinds of Asian food. It is also very useful as a standby for adding to any recipe that requires fresh ginger.

6 oz. fresh ginger

1 heaping teaspoon salt

¾ cup rice vinegar

2½ tablespoons sugar

1 small, clean, dry, warm jar with lid

MAKES ⅔ CUP

Choose nicely rounded pieces of ginger root. Separate the root into "lumps" and peel them. Rub the lumps with salt and leave in a covered bowl overnight.

Put the vinegar, ¾ cup water, and sugar in a bowl. Stir to dissolve.

Slice the ginger as thinly as possible, blanch quickly in boiling water, and dry on paper towels.

Fill a clean jar with ginger pieces and top with the vinegar marinade. Seal the jar. The pickle will be ready for use immediately and will keep well in the refrigerator after opening.

Note Ginger turns yellow when blanched and pink when pickled. If you have problems finding rice vinegar with the other vinegars, you'll find it near the sushi ingredients in the supermarket or at a natural food store. Try using white wine vinegar or dry sherry instead.

Indian green mango chutney

1 onion (4 oz.), cut into quarters

2–5 green and red chiles (to taste), halved and seeded

1 egg-size piece of fresh ginger, peeled and cut into quarters

2 garlic cloves, peeled

2 tablespoons mixed mustard seeds

1 tablespoon cumin seeds

2 teaspoons ground turmeric

½ teaspoon salt

1 cup white wine vinegar

1 tablespoon olive oil

½ cup sugar

1½ lb. green mangoes or other underripe fruit, cut into ½-inch cubes

4 pickle jars, ½ pint each, with screw bands and new lids, sterilized (page 7)

MAKES 1 QUART

This recipe is based on a traditional Indian pickle in which the spices and onion are reduced to a paste, then cooked in vinegar. The sugar and fruit are added toward the end and simmered just for a short while. Traditionally, hard green fruit is used, so try to find a hard mango rather than a ripe one. If ripe fruits are used, they will disintegrate too much and the idea is that the pickled fruit should retain its texture. Green or unripe papaya, peach, pear, quince, and garden japonica can be also be used to make this recipe. Try preserving green beans this way too. The chutney goes well with spiced stir-fries and casseroles, roast meats, curries, and Indian takeout. You could also try it with baked potato and scrambled eggs.

Put the onion, chiles, ginger, garlic, mustard and cumin seeds, turmeric, and salt in a blender and grind to a paste with 2–3 tablespoons of the vinegar.

Put the oil in a pan and cook the paste over low heat for 10 minutes, adding the remaining vinegar as the paste cooks down. Add the sugar and continue cooking over low heat until dissolved.

Add the fruit to the pan, stir well, and simmer until just tender but not soft, about 10 minutes. Spoon the chutney into the hot jars, leaving ½ inch headroom. Wipe the rims with a damp paper towel and cap the jars. Process for 15 minutes in a boiling-water bath (page 8). Let cool, label, and store in a cool, dark pantry until required.

Grannie's apple chutney

My mother's chutney was renowned—so delicious that any other chutney paled into insignificance and still does. It was originally an old country recipe passed on to her by Mother Haywood, the elderly mother of the licensee of a local pub. A recipe is kept alive by a new owner and thus changes name. In her later years, we all called my mother "Grannie," so now it is her chutney. The best thing is, like most chutneys, it is very simple to make. Serve in pork sandwiches, with all kinds of eggs, cheese, cold cuts, or with a hearty breakfast.

Chop the apples and onions very finely—this can be done in a food processor, but take care not to reduce it a pulp. It is important for the chutney to have texture.

Put the apples, onions, raisins, golden raisins, sugar, cayenne, mustard, ginger, salt, and the 2 cups malt vinegar in a large pan and simmer for 1–1½ hours over low to medium heat. Stir regularly to make sure the sugar does not burn, adding extra vinegar as necessary as the chutney reduces.

Turn off the heat and let the chutney settle. Stir and ladle into hot jars, leaving ½ inch headroom. Wipe the rims with a damp paper towel and cap the jars. Process for 10 minutes in a boiling-water bath (page 8).

Keep at least 1 month before you try it. This kind of chutney improves with age.

2 lb. tart apples, such as Granny Smith, peeled and cored

1 lb. onions, quartered

⅔ cup raisins

⅔ cup golden raisins

2½ cups soft brown sugar

½ teaspoon cayenne pepper

½ teaspoon hot powdered mustard

½ teaspoon ground ginger

1½ tablespoons salt

2 cups malt or cider vinegar, plus 2 cups extra to add as the chutney boils down

3-5 pickle jars, 1 pint each, with screw bands and new lids, sterilized (page 7)

MAKES 3-5 PINTS

Pumpkin and red tomato chutney

There are many varieties of pumpkin and this recipe can be used to preserve all of them. Make sure that the flesh is firm and not stringy, or it will spoil the finished texture of the chutney. I like to cut the pumpkin by hand into ½-inch cubes, so it retains its color and texture. If you are making large quantities, you may prefer to chop the vegetables in a food processor. You can also use other vegetables such as squash, zucchini, eggplant, unripe melons, and green tomatoes to make this recipe. Serve with bread and cheese, scrambled eggs, or cold cuts.

Put the pumpkin, tomato, onion, golden raisins, sugar, salt, ginger, garlic, nutmeg, and the 1 cup vinegar in a pan and bring slowly to a boil. Simmer for 1 hour, stirring from time to time. The chutney should look dark, dense, and rich. Add extra vinegar if the chutney dries out too much while cooking.

Transfer to the hot jar, leaving ½ inch headspace. Wipe the rim clean with a damp paper towel and cap the jar. Process for 10 minutes in a boiling-water bath (page 8). Label when cool and store for 1–6 months in a cool, dark pantry before opening.

1 lb. peeled and seeded firm pumpkin or butternut squash flesh, cut into ½-inch cubes

1 large ripe tomato, peeled, seeded, and chopped (1 cup)

1 large onion, chopped (1 cup)

⅔ cup golden raisins

1¼ cups soft brown sugar

1 teaspoon salt

1 inch fresh ginger, peeled and finely chopped

1 garlic clove, finely chopped

a little freshly grated nutmeg

1 cup malt vinegar, plus ½ cup extra

1 pickle jar, 1 pint, with screw band and new lid, sterilized (page 7)

MAKES 1 PINT

Williamsburg
sweet watermelon rind pickle

14 oz. watermelon rind
(2 cups after
preparation)

⅔ cup white vinegar

1 cup sugar

5 whole cloves

½ inch cinnamon stick

½ inch piece of fresh
ginger, crushed

a fluted or frilled
pastry wheel

a spice ball or
cheesecloth bag tied
with string

2 pickle jars, ½ pint
each, with screw bands
and new lids, sterilized
(page 7)

MAKES 1 PINT.

I was drawn to this old Virginian recipe simply because of the idea of turning those hefty wedges of peel left after a feast of watermelon into something delicious. It is a reminder of the very essence of all preserving; nothing was ever wasted if it could be turned into something wonderful, something readymade to keep in the pantry to pep up otherwise dreary winter food. Imagine when there was no readymade food at all—how welcome a jar of pickle would have been. The finished pickle is a lovely, soft, dark green and you may be surprised how much flavor watermelon rind has. Eat it with any cured, boiled, or baked ham and try it with cheese. Or just eat it from the spoon.

Using the pastry wheel, cut the watermelon rind into tiny squares. Put in a bowl, add the white vinegar and ½ cup water, cover, and let stand overnight.

Next morning, put the pieces of rind in a jelly bag or strainer and let drain for 2 hours or until quite dry. Discard the liquid. Transfer the rind to paper towels to absorb any remaining moisture.

To make the syrup, put the sugar and 2 cups water in a pan. Put the cloves, cinnamon, and ginger in a spice ball or tie in a cheesecloth bag and attach it to the handle of the pan so the spices are suspended in the syrup. Heat slowly to simmering point to dissolve the sugar, then boil for 10 minutes. Add the melon rind and simmer for 3 minutes.

Scoop out the rind with a perforated skimmer and put in the hot jars. Keep boiling the syrup until it has thickened, then pour it over the rind leaving ¼ inch headroom. Wipe the rims with a damp paper towel and cap the jars. Process for 10 minutes in a boiling-water bath (page 8). Let cool, then label.

Store in a dark pantry for 1 month before tasting—invert the jar from time to time to make sure the sugar does not crystallize on the base.

index

apples:
apple jelly with lemon
and sage, 22
Grannie's apple chutney,
59
pineapple and apple jam,
18
apricot conserve, dried, 11

berries:
cranberry relish with
orange zest, cinnamon,
and port, 33
hedgerow gin, 47
red berry jelly, 26
brandy:
ginger and juniper
liqueur, 44
layered "white" fruits in
brandy, 35
orange shrub, 42
peach halves in brandy
with star anise, 36

chutney, Indian green
mango, 57
chunky lemon, lime, and
grapefruit marmalade,
30
chutney:
Grannie's apple chutney,
59
Indian green mango
chutney, 57
pumpkin and red tomato
chutney, 60
conserves:
dried apricot, 11
Italian fig, 14
country bounce, 46
crabapple jelly, 25
cranberry relish with
orange zest, cinnamon,
and port, 33

Dolly's strawberry jam, 13
dried apricot conserve, 11

fig conserve, Italian, 14

gin, hedgerow, 47
ginger:
ginger and juniper liqueur,
44
Japanese pickled ginger,
55
pickled pears with
tamarind and ginger, 39
rhubarb and ginger jam,
21
Grannie's apple chutney, 59

grapefruit marmalade,
chunky lemon, lime,
and, 30
grappa:
ginger and juniper
liqueur, 44
kumquat and saffron
rosolio, 43
layered summer fruits in,
35
limoncello, 41
greengage jam, 17

hedgerow gin, 47

Indian green mango
chutney, 57
Italian fig conserve, 14

jam:
Dolly's strawberry jam, 12
greengage jam, 17
pineapple and apple jam,
18
rhubarb and ginger jam,
21
strawberry jam with
balsamic vinegar, 13
jam, jelly, and marmalade
making explained, 7
filling jars, 8
pectin, 7
pre-cooking the fruit, 8
processing jars in a
boiling-water bath, 8
sugar, 7
setting, 7
testing for set, 8
skimming, 8
yield, 8
jams, jellies, and
marmalades, 10–33
Japanese pickled ginger, 55
jellies:
apple jelly with lemon
and sage, 22
crabapple jelly, 25
red berry jelly, 26
kumquats:
kumquat and saffron
rosolio, 43
orange and kumquat
marmalade, 29

layered pickled vegetables,
49
layered summer fruits in
grappa, 35
lemon:
apple jelly with lemon
and sage, 22

chunky lemon, lime, and
grapefruit marmalade,
30
limoncello 41
Moroccan preserved
lemons and limes in salt,
51
limes:
chunky lemon, lime, and
grapefruit marmalade,
30
Moroccan preserved
lemons and limes in salt,
51
limoncello, 41
liqueurs, 40–47
ginger and juniper
liqueur, 44
liqueur making explained,
9

mangoes, Indian green
mango chutney, 57
marmalades:
chunky lemon, lime, and
grapefruit marmalade,
30
orange and kumquat
marmalade, 29
Seville orange
marmalade, 30
Mediterranean vegetables
in oil, 49
Moroccan preserved lemons
and limes in salt, 51

onions, Winter's farm
pickled, 52
oranges:
and kumquat marmalade,
29
orange shrub, 42
Seville orange
marmalade, 30

peach halves in brandy
with star anise, 36
pears, pickled, with
tamarind and ginger,
39
pickled pears with tamarind
and ginger, 39
pickles and chutneys,
48–63
pickle and chutney
making explained,
9
pickles:
Japanese pickled ginger,
55
layered pickled
vegetables, 49
pickled pears with
tamarind and ginger,
39

Williamsburg sweet
watermelon rind pickle,
63
Winter's farm pickled
onions, 52
pineapple and apple jam,
18
plums:
country bounce, 46
greengage jam, 17
Victoria plum jam, 17
preserve, fresh apricot, 11
preserved fruits, 34–39
preserved fruits explained,
9
preserving: general
preserving explained, 6
equipment, 6
fruit and vegetables, 6
hygiene, 7
jars, 7
preparing jars for
canning, 7
quantities, 6
pumpkin and red tomato
chutney, 60

raspberry and rhubarb jam,
21
rhubarb and ginger jam, 21
rosolio, kumquat, and
saffron, 43
rum:
country bounce, 46
orange shrub, 42

Seville orange marmalade,
30
shrub, orange, 42
strawberries:
Dolly's strawberry jam,
13
red berry jelly, 26
strawberry jam with
balsamic, 13
strawberry jam with
balsamic, 13

tomatoes: pumpkin and red
tomato chutney, 60

vegetables:
layered pickled, 49
Mediterranean
vegetables in oil, 49
Victoria plum jam, 17

watermelon: Williamsburg
sweet watermelon rind
pickle, 63
Williamsburg sweet
watermelon rind pickle,
63
Winter's farm pickled
onions, 52

conversion charts

Weights and measures have been rounded up
or down slightly to make measuring easier.

Volume equivalents:

American	Metric	Imperial
1 teaspoon	5 ml	
1 tablespoon	15 ml	
¼ cup	60 ml	2 fl.oz.
⅓ cup	75 ml	2 ½ fl.oz.
½ cup	125 ml	4 fl.oz.
⅔ cup	150 ml	5 fl.oz. (¼ pint)
¾ cup	175 ml	6 fl.oz.
1 cup	250 ml	8 fl.oz.

Weight equivalents: Measurements:

Imperial	Metric	Inches	cm
1 oz.	25 g	¼ inch	5 mm
2 oz.	50 g	½ inch	1 cm
3 oz.	75 g	¾ inch	1.5 cm
4 oz.	125 g	1 inch	2.5 cm
5 oz.	150 g	2 inches	5 cm
6 oz.	175 g	3 inches	7 cm
7 oz.	200 g	4 inches	10 cm
8 oz. (½ lb.)	250 g	5 inches	12 cm
9 oz.	275 g	6 inches	15 cm
10 oz.	300 g	7 inches	18 cm
11 oz.	325 g	8 inches	20 cm
12 oz.	375 g	9 inches	23 cm
13 oz.	400 g	10 inches	25 cm
14 oz.	425 g	11 inches	28 cm
15 oz.	475 g	12 inches	30 cm
16 oz. (1 lb.)	500 g		
2 1b.	1 kg		

Oven temperatures:

110°C	(225°F)	Gas ¼
120°C	(250°F)	Gas ½
140°C	(275°F)	Gas 1
150°C	(300°F)	Gas 2
160°C	(325°F)	Gas 3
180°C	(350°F)	Gas 4
190°C	(375°F)	Gas 5
200°C	(400°F)	Gas 6
220°C	(425°F)	Gas 7
230°C	(450°F)	Gas 8
240°C	(475°F)	Gas 9